The Arrogance

Tom Wise

Published by University of Truth
Mills River, NC

http://www.universityoftruth.org

Printed in the United States of America
First Printing, 2010

http://www.universityoftruth.org

INTRODUCTION

The purpose of this essay is to examine the deification of Jesus Christ. This is a primary cause, for whether His deification comes by self-appointment or by coronation from other men, the idea carries with it such enormous ramifications that to accept it is to relinquish one's entire life to it. But what if this acceptance is without firm basis? What if it is unwarranted? Then, obviously, deification of Jesus Christ is idolatry, a grave sin. It is therefore imperative that with a mind towards ultimate Truth, and with a heart open to right over wrong, we investigate fully whether Christ should be deified.

If the root of the idea for a deified Christ is based on feelings (for example, on heartfelt love for Him), this root is unsound if there is no more to support that emotion. In such case, the deification is only from personal belief, and is therefore subjective. If the concept is founded on established (church) doctrines, especially those upheld by mysterious and lengthy explanations and apologetics, they are at minimum suspect, at maximum quite against the teachings of Jesus. There must be clear basis for belief, not only faith in aggregate opinion or, worse, surrender to one's own overwhelming ignorance. We must have Truth.

This Truth is not accidental, nor is it obfuscated, but is able to be discovered and verified. Therefore, let us discover and verify.

Our sources for the Truth in this matter shall be the four Gospels[1] of Matthew, Mark, Luke, and John, all information from which we shall verify through Torah, the Law of God. This combination provides the proper lens by which we shall measure the words and deeds of Christ, or

[1] On certain points, the Gospels cannot agree with themselves, that is, are not synoptic, and we approach with that knowledge.

any doctrines of men which refer to Christ, to determine whether they are correct or incorrect.

Why is Torah the standard and light by which such verification shall take place? Jesus asserted that we must judge not Him personally but His works, that is, whether or not they are of the Father (John 10:37-38). Clearly, in order to judge whether His works are of the Father, there is no more visible or appropriate measure than Torah, given by God our Father. Indeed, what other yardstick from the Father exists? Thus, Christ could not issue such a spiritual challenge to His words and deeds without an expectation that such challenge would come by comparison to Torah. In this, Jesus was adhering to the Hebraic mindset, a paradigm which recognizes Torah to be the mirror by which ultimate Truth should be discerned, and the filter by which it may be extracted[2].

The Gospels contain the core material for knowing Jesus Christ. While evident that their respective authors (especially John) included a certain amount of "spin," the Gospels are the most complete and, conceivably, the most accurate accounts of Christ's words and deeds. To disown the Gospels for any spin would therefore be a deliberate attempt to avoid best endeavor, preventing us from even attempting this essay.

In establishing any truthful thing concerning Jesus Christ, we shall not often, if at all, utilize writings from any other Christian theologian or historian, even that most notable, Paul. Why? Simply and directly, such writings, whether or not inspired, are opinion and commentary on the Truth, and therefore not fit for foundation. Such "external" material may, however, be employed for secondary concurrence but only if it agrees first with the Hebraic mindset. We believe this limits as much as possible

[2] In a larger context, the Hebraic mindset also reads the entire Bible as Jews (or Hebrews) speaking to Jews (or those otherwise curious and/or zealous) about Torah (or, in a cultural/ethnic manner, Jewish) matters.

the intrusion of weaker ideas and doctrine. Some will argue that it is impossible to understand the Gospels without first consulting the epistles of Paul, but we think this Paulian approach to be self-serving, laying, or appearing to lay, more validity on latter-day doctrines than on foundational truths, a grave error. For if the Gospels, through presentation of Christ's life and death, passed through the lens of Torah, can without doubt indicate that Christ should be deified, all doctrine which follows such a conclusion must be validated. If, however, no such Truth can be derived by this highest method, any other attempt to deify Christ must be considered of men, and therefore incorrect. The mirror argument, that our barrier to Paulian understanding is likewise self-serving, only means to wrestle our previous argument to a stalemate, but it cannot overcome the necessity for Truth to precede doctrine.

In keeping with this spirit of primary origination, we likewise shall not commonly consult with interpretations from the Jewish Sages (for example, from Talmud). In this, we have three reasons. First, there is a matter of fair concordance. That is, if we shall not permit Christian doctrine to color our thinking, we ought not lean too heavily upon Jewish doctrine. Second, we prefer the simpler explications. While it may on the surface appear that the deification of Jesus Christ is a subject of great complexity, the demand of the doctrine, that it be understood by those without too much biblical knowledge, especially by children and (literal) idiots, challenges all to demystify it or else appear involved with intellectual intimidation, leading to congregations filled with the confused. This we hope to avoid, if not dismantle. Third, Jewish conclusions concerning Christ have their own prejudices. One prejudice is that the deifying doctrines of Protestant and Catholic Christianity automatically stifle and negate any discourse into His righteousness. This is due to the perception of Christian idolatry. Another prejudice is that the history of Christianity has for seventeen or more centuries been filled with every type of persecution against the Jews, in the name of Christ. This has caused reluctance of Jewish relationship with both

Christianity and Jesus Christ. But while the aforementioned are valid reasons for prejudicial Jewish opinions against Christ and Christianity, they nevertheless are slanted and therefore not generally conducive to true ends.

Our investigation will not exhaust every perspective. Such is neither possible nor productive. Instead, we shall walk those avenues which in our opinion properly represent the major views and beliefs pertaining to the deification of Christ. In such, the Christian doctrine will be amply displayed but also frequently challenged. Nevertheless, some areas may go unexplored if we believe sufficient and incontrovertible evidence on a particular point has been otherwise presented. This is neither injudicious nor malicious, but a concentration, if not a necessary limitation.

In sum, our aim is to prove or disprove whether Jesus Christ ought to be deified. This we will accomplish using an Hebraic mindset, first by accepting Torah as the foundation for all Truth, second by confirming the Gospels through comparison with Torah, and third by examining doctrine in relation to the first two.

WARNINGS AGAINST DEIFICATION

Advancing any person to the status of God (by which we mean the Supreme Being, who was antecedent to the material universe as we know it) is a risky venture, to say the least. Concerning such deification, there are a number of biblical warnings already in place:

(1) Torah (Numbers 23:19) states explicitly that God is not a man, nor is He the son of man. This alone is a strong argument against any countervailing doctrine.

(2) The First Commandment (Exodus 20:3) places God above all things, and Torah (Deuteronomy 6:4) makes it clear that God is singular. Therefore, there is only One, and One is unmatched. No man may thus ascend.

(3) The Second Commandment (Exodus 20:4-5) makes it a capital crime to create a graven image or any likeness of any thing "in the earth beneath" to which one might give veneration, bowing or serving. If a man is deified, any likeness or image of that man is an idol. A vehement argument here is that God alone is exempt from this ban, so that any graven image or likeness of the true God should be permissible, even acceptable. However, supposing this argument adheres to the letter of the Law, and that we are not disallowed from creating an image or likeness of the one true God, who can say what is God's image or likeness? Obviously, no one. Any such representation comes only from opinion and belief, not fact, and therefore constitutes an idol. Since it is impossible to know, it is forbidden to create. A weaker argument is that God created us "in His image," and therefore we all in some manner represent a likeness of God. But are we all God? Of course not.

(4) The expulsion from Eden (Genesis 3:22-23) was at least partly due to God's decision that man should not equal God in His immortality.

(5) The confounding of language at the Tower of Babel (Genesis 11:1-9) was at least partly due to man's arrogance, believing himself able to reach the heaven of God.

(6) Man's humility is commanded as a basic tenet in our relationship to and with Him (Deuteronomy 10:12, Micah 6:8).

Clearly, God has not granted permission to deify any man, and in fact has forbidden it.

IGNORING THE WARNINGS

If one ignores or otherwise reinterprets all of the aforementioned biblical bans and warnings in order to therefore deify a man, this is sin.

But if for some reason sin is waved off, the deified man may be challenged on other grounds, such as through (1) determining whether or not certain of his words, deeds, or qualities deemed to be godlike are in fact unique, or even godlike, and (2) deductive reasoning, that is, logic. These we shall incorporate into our investigation following.

TYPES OF EVIDENCE

Concerning the deity of Christ, we will reduce all evidence into two categories: (1) circumstantial evidence, and (2) confessional evidence. By circumstantial evidence, we mean those actions of Christ which appear or have been made to appear godlike. By confessional evidence, we mean those words from Jesus Christ which might be considered self-deification.

CIRCUMSTANTIAL EVIDENCE

CIRCUMSTANTIAL EVIDENCE: INTRODUCTION

Circumstantial evidence falls under two headings, "pro" and "con." Pro denotes circumstantial evidence which gives credence to the deification of Christ, while con, of course, rejects that deification. Our goal here is twofold: (1) to discover whether there are inconsistencies in the pro circumstantial evidence, and (2) to discover whether con circumstantial evidence is strong enough to reject the deification of Jesus.

CIRCUMSTANTIAL EVIDENCE: PRO

Pro circumstantial evidence shall be broken into seven subheadings: (1) healing, (2) pre-crucifixion miracles other than healing, (3) prophecy, (4) doctrines, (5) personal sacrifices, (6) resurrection, and (7) ascension.

1. Healing

The power to heal is a marvelous gift, but does it prove a man to be a deity? Jesus healed many, but He ordered also that the apostles "heal the sick, cleanse the lepers" (Matthew 10:8), and "cure diseases" (Luke 9:1). Indeed, the apostles were able to heal (Luke 9:6), and we know at least one specific thing, that Peter healed a lame man (Acts 3:1-10). In Tanakh (Old Testament), Elisha had the power to cure Naaman's leprosy (2 Kings Chapter 5). If Christ is deified by the power of healing, are Peter and Elisha likewise deified? If not, why is Christ?

2. Pre-Crucifixion Miracles Other than Healing

Besides healing, Jesus performed other miracles, such as turning water into wine, calming a storm, walking on water, casting out devils, resurrecting Lazarus, "transfiguring," and defeating Satan's temptations (and this list is not complete). Yet each of these is problematic in deciding for Christ's deification.

First, let us examine the turning of water into wine, comparing it to a like miracle from Moses. At a marriage feast to which Christ and His disciples were invited, Jesus did so to please his mother (John 2:1-12). In the wilderness, for the children of Israel, Moses brought forth water from a rock (Numbers 20:2-11). Although not identical, these two miracles seem similar in nature (the transmutation of physical objects) and purpose (to slake the thirst of many, and to show the power of God), enough to say that Christ's miracle was not unique, therefore providing no reason for His deification.

Second, let us examine Christ calming the storm, comparing this to an incident with Jonah. Jesus did so to calm the fears of His apostles in their battered ship (Mark 4:35-41). Jonah knew that if he were cast into the sea, a raging storm would cease to batter his shipmates (Jonah 1:11-15). While their respective storms ceased for different reasons, the resulting lessons in faith and purpose (Mark 4:40-41, Jonah 1:16) are similar, enough to say that Christ's miracle was not unique, therefore providing no reason for His deification.

Third, let us examine Christ walking on water (Matthew 14:22-33), comparing this to Moses parting the Red Sea. Here, we find Christ performing an act which is singular. For though Torah states specifically that the Hebrews trod on dry land between halves of the receded Red Sea (Exodus chapter 14), no one walked upon the water. But Jesus did. In this case, Christ's miracle does seem to advance the notion of His deification. However, there is a small caveat to this conclusion, being that Peter also walked a little on the waves (Matthew 14:29)[3]. Furthermore, we may employ some practical skepticism, for in modern times we have seen fakirs and fakers perform similarly. In conclusion, we cannot say that Christ walking on water provides a reason for His deification, only that it lends a mark in the pro column.

Fourth, let us examine the casting out of devils. Here, we come upon the same dilemma facing the power of healing, which is that Christ ordained the apostles also to "cast out devils" (Matthew 10:8) and that they were capable of such things (Mark 6:13). Indeed, "the seventy" had such power (Luke 10:17). To cast out devils does not prove deity.

Fifth, let us examine the power of Jesus Christ to three times resurrect the dead: **(1)** Christ raised his uncle, Lazarus, brother to Mary and Martha

[3] It may be argued that Peter did not actually take steps to travel but merely placed his feet into the sea, thinking he would float above. It is admitted that he sank almost immediately.

(John 11:1-44). However, Jesus petitioned God for this ability (11:40-41), which speaks more for the power of God than for the power of Christ. **(2)** Christ brought back the daughter of Jairus, a ruler of the synagogue at Capernaum (Mark 5:21-43). Yet, it is not clear whether the girl was truly dead or if in a "sleeping" state that simulated death, perhaps in a coma (5:39). **(3)** Most credible, Jesus revived the widow's son, clearly dead (Luke 7:11-17). This He did with few words or pomp, Christ more "godlike" than during the resurrection of Lazarus. Nevertheless, according to the crowd that witnessed this resurrection, "a great prophet is risen up among us" and "God hath visited his people" (7:16), both of which ambiguous praises must be understood from the Hebraic mindset. Supposing, on the other hand, these Jews meant by their cheering to deify Christ, that still is not proof of His godhood, only of their mistake.

Beyond these constructionist doubts lies the disconcerting reality that Christ was not unique in His power to resurrect. Elijah the Prophet also raised a young boy from the dead (1 Kings 17:17-24), and the apostles were given the same power (Matthew 10:8)[4]. Since Jesus was not the only person to ever successfully command the dead to rise, He cannot be deified by that power.

Sixth, let us examine the transfiguration (Matthew 17:1-13, Mark 9:2-13, Luke 9:28-36): **(1)** Immediately, we come upon the odd fact that John the apostle was present on the mountain, yet the Book of John does not mention this momentous occasion at all, which seems strange since John is the apostle most eager to glorify Christ. **(2)** Next, Christ was "transfigured before them and his face did shine as the sun, and his raiment was white as the light" (Matthew 17:2). However, I think this compares closely with the shining face of Moses (Exodus 34:29-30), who also was so very close to God that he absorbed and radiated His glory. This similarity is noted (albeit under different doctrine) by Paul (2

---

[4] Even Paul possibly brought Eutychus back to life (Acts 20:9-12).

Corinthians 3:7-13). The net result is a stumbling-block to the deification of Jesus. **(3)** Following His transfiguration, Christ met with Moses and Elijah on the mountaintop[5]. This, however, was a meeting of peers, for all three great prophets "appeared in glory" (Luke 9:30-31), further dissolving the idea that Christ was unique. **(4)** After this, they "spake of his decease which he should accomplish at Jerusalem" (9:31). But this is puzzling in several ways. Why should they discuss the "decease" of a deity? What input could Moses and Elijah offer not already known to a deity? If Jesus is a deity, why did He meet with Moses and Elijah on a mountaintop rather than in lofty chambers? **(5)** Finally, the futility in deifying Christ becomes clear when God proclaims, "This is my Beloved Son: hear him" (Luke 9:35), verifying that Christ is the Son of God, not God. Ignoring for the moment the immediate compulsion of the Christian to incorporate the Son of God into a triad, a Trinity, we must confront that, throughout the Bible, God has called others His son, indicating that "Son of God" is not quite a unique honor. Further muddying the waters, God calls both Israel (Exodus 3:22) and Ephraim (Jeremiah 31:9) his *firstborn* son. Are Israel and Ephraim the same entity? Where does that leave Jesus Christ? But if the argument is that Christ is the "only *begotten* Son" (John 3:16), how can a firstborn son (Israel, Ephraim) not also be a begotten son? Have we not stretched beyond our own understanding? In so saying, there is provided no clear reason for deifying Christ.

Concluding on the transfiguration, I think it evident that the meeting between Christ, Moses, and Elijah contains a great many obstacles to faith in the deity of Christ. At most, Jesus is shown to be a little above the level of Moses and Elijah.

---

[5] While the appearance of Moses has a connection to Moses' own transfiguration (Exodus), the appearance of Elijah is connected to his translation (see "7. Ascension").

Seventh, let us examine Jesus Christ defeating Satan's temptations (Matthew 4:1-11). To begin, we cannot say that Jesus performed any miracles at that moment, for there are none to see. Instead, Christ, by His willpower, faith in God, and knowledge in Torah, withstood many seductions. Yet it is this very thing, that Satan tempted Christ at all, which is a great impediment to His deification.

According to the doctrine of Trinitarian Christianity, the Son of God is the same as God, Christ being "very God of very God, being of one substance (homoousios) with the Father." So, let us ask, Does God need to be fed, or to be preserved from harm? Of course not. Does God not already reign over every part of the Earth? Yes, He does. If the Trinitarian doctrine is correct, what then did Satan offer to Jesus Christ which was not already His? Naturally, nothing. The Trinitarian doctrine therefore fails this test.

Obviously, Satan did not believe that He was tempting God but rather the Son of God, who is evidently of a different nature and will than God. For not only did the adversary tempt Jesus, but he believed the Son of God's allegiance susceptible to a satanic promise of earthly power (Matthew 4:8-10). Such would not be possible if Christ and God were of the same substance. Jesus is by this shown to be separate from God, and not God. Shall we say that Christ was *not* able to be tempted? What then the drama? Where then Christ's victory? It would all be just boring eventuality. But if Jesus is not God, being different from God, all the drama and victory returns, and happily so, though the doctrine of Trinity fails.

It might be argued that Satan did not know Jesus was God "in the flesh." If this is true, our adversary may be dismissed as weak, without a great power of perception, and not prince of the air. However, I think we know that Satan is strong. It might also be argued that Satan *did* know Jesus was God in the flesh, but pursued his fruitless mission anyway. If this is true, our adversary is ridiculous. Knowing that God could never be tempted by those temptations which were offered to Christ, we may call Satan, with no slim chance to bend God to his will, unintelligent. However, I think we know the devil is both knowledgeable and crafty, the most intelligent adversary. Logically, Satan knew *exactly* who he tempted, and that it was not, could not be, God. Factually, he called Jesus "Son of God" and not God. These things are clear impediments to the deification of Jesus Christ.

Christ was able to be swayed but He did not waver. Why? The credit is due completely to the strength of Torah, from which Jesus quoted three times (from Deuteronomy 8:3, 6:16, and 10:20), once for each temptation. Shall anyone suggest otherwise, that Christ's use of Torah was not the ultimate solution to a tense crossroads but only was a wry smile from deity to believer? Such is illogical, indicating some necessity to second-guess clear meanings. Torah, that most excellent shield, deflected the temptations to the flesh of Jesus Christ. This fact is another stumbling-block to the deification of Christ.

3. Prophecy

Jesus was a true prophet, according to the standards of Torah, a prophet of the Lord God and no other god. He furthermore spoke with accuracy concerning future events, such as the coming destruction of the Temple and dispersal of the Jews (John 4:21-24). However, there have been other prophets of equal stature, notably Moses and Isaiah. Therefore, the power to prophecy, even to great magnitude, does not denote deity.

Christ in fact asserted His own limitations, saying of the end time that no man, no angel, not even the Son knows the hour or day, but only the Father knows (Mark 13:32). This is another glaring obstacle to the deification of Jesus Christ.

4. The Doctrines of Christ

The Law of God, Torah, is immutable, as it is written (Deuteronomy 4:2). Therefore, any person who would claim the authority to alter the Law of God in any way is not His representative. In fact, Jesus correctly asserted that *anyone* who would teach to break the least commandment shall be called "least" in the kingdom of heaven (Matthew 5:19). Christian doctrine, however, states that Jesus Christ by His crucifixion and/or resurrection somehow changed Torah, or upended the rules for obedience to it. If this is true, Christ would be not worthy for anything, let alone deification. He instead would be "least." We must therefore decide between Christ and this Christian doctrine. Since Christ agrees with Torah, the choice is simple - it is this Christian doctrine which is incorrect, breeding these least!

Did Jesus live up to His own standard? Or, during His lifetime, did Christ ever teach against, or exemplify to avoid, any least commandment of Torah? No, He did not.

First, He stated that He came not to destroy the Law of God, and specified clearly that He harbored no intention to alter Torah in any way, not a letter nor a portion of a letter of it, not a "jot" or a "tittle" (Matthew 5:17-18). So armed with this fact, we assume always the doctrines of Christ to be in every way congruent with Torah. Were some Jews "astonished" at His doctrine? Yes (Matthew 7:28-29), but we cannot attribute this to His aberration from the Law, only to His great understanding of it. In fact, unless one is deliberately seeking to undermine Him without thought to defend, Christ's actions cannot be shown to have overstepped Torah.

Second, that the Pharisees sought to catch Jesus in an unlawful act is not an indictment that He ever acted against Torah. Rather, He was a target of consequence for them. According to many Jewish Sages, this "sinat hinam" ("baseless hatred" or, in this context, "Jew baselessly hating Jew") was the major cause for God allowing the destruction of the Second Temple[6]. The Pharisees were in fact so desperate to condemn Christ that many false witnesses were permitted to testify against Him (Matthew 26:60). Jewish scholars reject this episode as falsehood, claiming that no such corrupt Sanhedrin ever existed, but the facts do not square with that rejection. Conclusively, either Jesus was a lawful Jew unfairly put to death, a symptom of historical sinat hinam, or else the Gospels lie. All things considered, we believe the Gospels truthful, that Christ was always righteous by the Law.

Supposing, however, Jesus to be God, would that give Him the authority to transgress any Torah commandment? If so, why did He explicitly say He would not, and that any who would are to be called least? If He did transgress any commandment, why so subtly that even a Sanhedrin zealous for His blood had trouble finding Him guilty?

Conversely, does it prove Jesus to be deified due to His great allegiance to Torah? If so, every righteous man is deified, but this is impossible. It might be argued that Christ was most righteous of all men, but this proves only His level of righteousness, and does not bestow any godhood.

Nevertheless, though always righteous, Jesus was not unique. For Enoch was another man of perfection (Genesis 5:24), and perhaps we might also include Caleb, Joshua, and Job on such a list. This is an obstacle to the deification of Christ.

5. The Personal Sacrifices of Christ

[6] New Testament amplifying that which Talmud identifies.

Concerning the personal sacrifices of Christ (mainly, His voluntary surrender to persecution and martyrdom), these are well-known. Yet, none have the power to deify Christ.

But if one says that Christ's death especially identifies Him as the "suffering servant" (Isaiah Chapter 53), this ought not be overstated, for the suffering servant is not a deified being, not even a particular man, but an abstract personification of he who bears the sin of his people, and not as a willing substitute for their punishment but as one righteous who is persecuted for no other reason than that he will allow the persecution. Indeed, Christ is one who suffered so, and therefore He *was* a suffering servant. However, Christian doctrine has elevated this idea of a "suffering servant" to an ideal beyond its intent, creating a stratum of interpretation which focuses too little on the sins of the people and too much on the forbearance of the servant. That is, the doctrine has so glorified the suffering servant that, when one says Christ suffered as a suffering servant, Christ is thus deified. Yet, the flaw here is apparent, for the intent of the description of the suffering servant is not to cause us to revere him as a god but to remind us how sinfully men take advantage of the weak, the meek, the humble, and the righteous, grinding down those who do not fight back. The suffering servant is one who ought *not* to exist, but does. He should not have to take one more spear but does so because we continue to act shamefully, that is, sin. Our shame is that the suffering servant exists at all, but Christian doctrine *celebrates* his existence!

In Christian doctrine, the suffering servant is the savior of the human race. That is, by taking on the sins of the people, he "cleanses" them. But this is not Truth. The suffering servant is not one who steps forward to pay for sin but simply says nothing to stop the sin which is perpetrated upon him. For some reason, however, this has caused Christians to conclude that the suffering servant is the Messiah, and that the tale of the suffering servant is a prophecy of Messiah, i.e., Jesus Christ. Surely,

Christ suffered many things, and perhaps even died in a similar manner to Isaiah's suffering servant, yet there are two things of which we ought to remain conscious: (1) Christ's manner was dissimilar to that of the suffering servant, for Jesus was not silent at every turn but spoke out incessantly over the injustices and corruptions of His day, and (2) even if the life of Christ exactly followed that of Isaiah's suffering servant, the one is not glorified by the other. They are not interchangeable for the purpose of deification.

Christ did not create the doctrine that the suffering servant, by his forbearance, takes away the punishment for sin. That is a fabrication of the Christian church. Christ's doctrine is more responsible, esteeming repentance for (Matthew 4:17) and "remission of" (Luke 24:47) sins, that is, "go and sin no more" (John 8:11). He never urged to rely upon the acts of another as a way of salvation. That is also a fabrication of the Christian church, a promise of eternal security in exchange for allegiance.

Christ never said that He was the suffering servant. He did, however, say that He should be likened to the brazen serpent, for "as Moses lifted up the serpent in the wilderness, even so must the Son of man be lifted up" (John 3:14). This "serpent in the wilderness" was a metallic snake on a pole which did, under the authority of God, save many Hebrews bitten by actual serpents (sent by God as punishment for their continued grumbling). By gazing at this metal serpent, their lives were spared (Numbers 21:2-9). Thus, according to *His* doctrine, Christ's crucifixion does not represent a suffering servant but instead a focal point for God's saving power, in the same manner as the brazen serpent.

But whether we say that His crucifixion reflects a suffering servant (shaky or false doctrine) or a disposition towards being a focal point for God's salvation (true doctrine), Jesus is not in either case deified by that crucifixion nor by His willingness to die. Martyrdom, even that which may appear to be unique, is not deification.

Christ is also not deified by any resulting influence after His crucifixion. Certainly, the Christian church deified Him and established the Christian religion, but religion is not an innate extension of God. Assuredly also, many have found salvation of the spirit by calling on Jesus Christ, but the ability to transform lives, to be influential, is not cause for deification, as that would be a form of idolatry.

The Purpose of Christ's Sacrifice

According to Jesus Christ, eternal life is received by keeping commandments (Matthew 19:16-18), that is, by adherence to Torah. In the judgment, many will look to Christ and say, "Lord, Lord, have we not prophesied in thy name? And in thy name have cast out devils? And in thy name done many wonderful works? And then will I profess unto them, I never knew you; depart from me, ye that work *iniquity*" (Matthew 7:22-23). Clearly, working iniquity (sin) causes one to become unrecognizable to the most righteous. Christians ought therefore to keep Torah to the extent to which it may apply (Acts 15:20-21, et al).

As a matter of Law, sin can only be attributed when a Torah commandment has been transgressed, that is, sin can only be imputed by Torah[7]. Any other definition of sin is a fantasy, a mere doctrine of men, for which there is no need to repent. Repentance, therefore, is a matter of cleansing transgression against Torah.

To truly repent is three steps: (1) to understand and regret one's sin, (2) to plead with remorse for God's forgiveness, and (3) to change the future by coming to obedience.

---

[7] Righteousness is likewise defined only by Torah. When one refrains from an evil forbidden as a negative commandment (for example, "Thou shalt not murder"), righteousness is fulfilled by fleeing from that evil (and the desire to commit it). The same fulfillment applies when one obeys a positive commandment (for example, "Remember the Sabbath").

Once repentance is accomplished, there is salvation for that sin. This repentance is the gospel of Christ (Matthew 4:17).

The Christian doctrine which states that mere acceptance of an idea[8] puts one under Christ's protection, and/or makes one untouchable as it concerns torment in the afterlife (that is, will save you), is a removal of the responsibility for one's action (that is, for transgression of negative commandments) and inaction (that is, for transgression of positive commandments). The truth is, you cannot be absolved from your punishment by hiding behind the righteousness of Christ. You must personally repent, and then personally return to obedience. The love of Christ is otherwise, as He said, not forthcoming. I will quote Wesley here: "On this condition, not otherwise. A thunderbolt for Antinomianism! Who then dares assert that God's love does not at all depend on man's works?"

What did Jesus say of His own death? Did He say that it pays for the punishment of sins, providing the pathway to eternal life? No, but, "Greater love hath no man than this, that a man lay down his life for his friends. Ye are my friends, if ye do whatsoever I command you" (John 15:13-14). If Jesus is God, His commandments are Torah (laying forth an imminent threat to Christian doctrine). If Jesus is not God, He cannot in any way create any new commandments, nor would He (all previously explained). Thus, "whatsoever I command you" can only be under the authority of Torah. Ergo, Jesus died not to resolve the punishment for sins but foundationally to defend Torah.

The Hebraic Mindset of Christ

Was Christ a Jew or was He not? He was, circumcised (Luke 2:21) and raised in the Law (2:41).

[8] The concept that Jesus died for the sins of the world, that is, for commutation of your sins.

Did he speak to His people? All Christ's apostles were Jews, and His intended audience was neither Gentile nor Samaritan but only the lost sheep of Israel (Matthew 10:5-6).

Did He speak of Torah things? Preaching, Christ taught that eternal life comes by obedience to commandments as well as by God's judgment and justice (Mark 10:17-19; cf. Revelation 22:12,14). He told His disciples to observe and do everything which the Pharisees and scribes commanded (Matthew 23:2-3), cognizant that Torah grants and endows the judges, Levites, and priests of Israel with great latitude of authority and lawful interpolation (Deuteronomy 17:9-13). His gospel was also Torah, announcing the power of repentance and the necessity to refrain from evil. When prosecuted, He was so righteous by the Law that the Sanhedrin felt compelled to bring false witnesses (Matthew 26:59). Jesus was a Torah Jew.

That most Christian hierarchies will not permit Christ to be so Jewish, or that most Jewish hierarchies will not allow for a Christ with such pedigree[9], does not change the fact that Jesus had a 100% Hebraic mindset.

6. The Resurrection of Christ

Does Christ's resurrection denote His deity? There are to such a proposition two glaring incongruities.

First, God cannot die, and therefore God cannot be resurrected. The entire scenario is implausible. How would God achieve His own death?

---

[9] Some Jews will not even admit for a righteous Christ, extending such negativity to portraying Him as a traitor or even a myth (many times even disallowing the mention of His name). This Jewish aim to protect itself from Christian doctrine, and from persecution, is, given history, a reasonable expectation.

How would God accomplish His resurrection if He were truly dead? It is impossible. God, who has no body, cannot die. No death, no resurrection.

Supposing, however, that God can make Himself to die, and furthermore has the power to self-resurrect, would it mean anything? Of course not! The purpose of (bodily) resurrection is to reward the righteous (Isaiah 26:19-20, et al). The so-called "resurrection of God" is a nullification of this hope for the sake of fanciful security. The resurrection of Christ, on the other hand, is hope incarnate, restoration in return for defending Torah to the death. Sound doctrine is therefore that God did not resurrect Himself but instead a well-deserving man was resurrected by God.

Christian doctrine opposes these truths, and furthermore claims that God both can and cannot die, a folly of two polar beliefs. The Christian justification that such things are "mysteries" is not conducive to simplicity or rationality. It follows therefore that, as a matter of fundamental reasoning and good sense, we must eliminate that Christian doctrine. However, because this doctrine is central to Christianity, we must deny not only the faulty claims but also the religion which surrounds such unreasonable positions. This we must do even if our lives be turned upside down. Not even for the sake of peaceful communion with fellows or to keep from personal change, being too fearful or sedentary, should we retreat backwards. Such emotional reactions must be avoided if we are to have sound religion.

Second, others (some described above) have been resurrected, but these are not deified by that action. It might be argued that Christ's three days of interment prove Him to be a special case. Granted, but our appreciation must be for His place as the first-fruits of the eternal resurrection (that is, never to die again), a state which many righteous will share in the world to come. This fact also disproves Christ's uniqueness, another check against His deification.

As to the phenomenon of resurrection itself, it is believed in various ways by most of the world's religions, in both bodily and spiritual resurrections, and in reincarnation. Of the arguments against resurrection, these are atheistic arguments, which have nothing invested in belief and everything vested in causing disbelief. But, to answer the charge against resurrection, I will use the atheist's argument "extraordinary claims require extraordinary evidence" to say that I think it extraordinary for the vast majority of humanity to believe in a phenomenon as unnatural as resurrection! Now, even if this does not prove resurrection, it does prove that humanity in general has specific needs which the belief in resurrection addresses. We should as human beings therefore ask where this need originates and why resurrection fills that need (but I think the answer is too metaphysical, and besides takes us off topic). Personally, I fully believe in the bodily resurrection, and in the non-deifying resurrection of Jesus Christ.

7. Ascension

Does Christ's ascension denote deity? It does not, for Elijah also ascended to heaven (2 Kings 2:1-12). But if this seems too abrupt a reply, it is only because ascension is of such supernatural stuff that I am only able to muster a brief yet valid insight.

8. Conclusion

The obstacles discovered by examination of pro circumstantial evidence are too many to overcome. By these results, Christ cannot be deified.

As a sidelight and adjunct, Moses freed the Hebrew slaves, parted the Red Sea, by some perception made manna fall from heaven, stayed with God forty days in Mt. Sinai, gave the Law of God to the Hebrews, and did many more epic feats. Yet no one deifies Moses.

CIRCUMSTANTIAL EVIDENCE: CON

Con circumstantial evidence will be divided into three sub-headings: (1) Son of God, Word of God, (2) repentance, and (3) prayer.

1. Son of God, Word of God

By way of introduction, let us observe that Christ is not called "God" by His apostles, but is called "Son of God." To those steeped in the Trinitarian Christian doctrine, who believe "Son of God" to be a euphemism for God, this distinction may seem inconsequential. However, at no time did the apostles approach Jesus Christ as deified. Instead, they followed Him as a master of Torah and philosophy, and were awed by His application of Zohar (the supernatural underpinning for the Law of God). They also found in Him an intentional proponent of individual valuation, an attitude missing from daily Temple life as administered by the Pharisees of Christ's time (this being a cause of so many "lost sheep of Israel"). Christ was their leader and their friend, a compatriot who loved them. To the apostles, Jesus was very much a human being, albeit one with great power and wisdom. "Son of God" as the apostles used the title has no relationship to the homoousios "Son of God" of Trinitarian Christian doctrine. Thus, our starting proposition is that Trinitarian Christianity kidnapped this true Son of God and replaced Him with the convenient and recognizable symbol He is today.

To begin, Christ, the Son of God is, according to the doctrine of John the apostle, equated with the Word (John 1:1). Now, the Word of God is Torah. Irrespective of attitudes, opinions, and preferences to the contrary, this is ironclad. For John was an apostle, not the master, and bound by that association to reflect only that which was of Christ. As previously detailed, Christ was in perfect alignment with Torah, in both word and deed. He battled Satan with Torah. He espoused the immutability of God's Law, warning those who would think to change any small bit. He was found without lawful fault before the Sanhedrin (but for the false accusation of blasphemy). Christ's "Word" was Torah, and therefore John's "Word" must be Torah. By this connection, the Son of God, who is Christ, who is the Word, is Torah. That is, Christ is Torah in the flesh.

Let us continue in this vein. According to Jewish doctrine, Torah (God's Word) created the universe. According to Christian doctrine, Christ (Son of God) created the universe. This mutual agreement of doctrines has that same Torah-Christ connection. But since doctrines are not sufficient for our investigation, we must return to Torah to uphold this idea rightly. Here we find that the universe[10] was created by God's *Word*, by His speech, for He said, "Let there be...", and there was. The connection between Torah-Christ-Word is thus retained.

How deep does it go? John wrote, "In the beginning was the Word, and the Word was with God, and the Word was God" (John 1:1). First, "in the beginning" is a relative term, signifying the onset of something, almost certainly the creation of the universe. At that beginning, we find the Word.

Second, "with God" seems to separate the Word from God. A singular object is not "with" itself. Only two or more objects may be "with" each other. However, since God is not an object, for He is limitless and without borders, all things are naturally "with" God, none truly separated (except perhaps those things God intentionally keeps separate). Nevertheless, I think "with God" does not denote physical proximity, but instead loyalty to God, that is, doing only God's bidding with no deviation between the Will of God and the will of the Word ("I'm *with* you"). That John says "*was* with God" gives pause, for there is the

---

[10] Perhaps it would be more accurate to say the *universes*, or perhaps the *dimensions*, for we know that God created not only the *earth*, i.e., *matter*, but also the *heaven*, i.e., the *spirit*, as well as that unique *Heaven* which is God's domain (Genesis 1:1-10).

appearance of a union dissolved, but in no case should we think the Word had gone adrift from God.

Third, most pertinent, "was God" uses the past tense, a glaring inconsistency towards deification of the Word. The immediate argument against this will be that I have excluded "the Word was with God" from the same regulation. Not so! For "was with God" does not indicate a fluctuating state of being, but "was God" does. That is, God's Word has been and always will remain loyal to God ("with God"), but it has changed from its original state. The original state of the Word was the *idea* of the Word. That is, before God *spoke* the Word He had to *conceive* the Word. When it was still an idea in the "mind" of God (that being God's essence), the Word was not only *with* God, but it also *was* God. When the idea of the Word was spoken, it was changed to its new and ultimate form (state). For our discussion, the two ultimate forms (states) of the Word which pertain are (1) the Torah given to Moses (if you will, "the Word made known") and (2) the man called Jesus Christ ("the Word made flesh"). These ultimate forms (states) of the Word are no longer in their original state, no longer God per se, but are outward expressions of God, separate from Him.

It might be argued, with great force, that the Word *is* God for continuing to effectuate the desires of God. Similarly, a father's verbal instruction to his child still effectuates his desires. Can the child say that the verbal instruction, the father's word, does not carry the same authority and therefore the desires of the father himself? Of course not. Nevertheless, no reasonable person would agree that the sound waves which emanated from the father's mouth are still part of the father (in this case, physically), only that they are (or were) *from* the father. The same applies to any ultimate state for the Word of God, whether Torah or Christ. They are *from* God, but not God, and deification is thus denied to both.

The Sons of God

When Jesus was in danger of stoning for blasphemy[11], He asked, "Is it not written in your law, I said, Ye are gods? If He called them gods, unto whom the word of God came, and the Scripture cannot be broken, say ye of Him, whom the Father hath sanctified, and sent into the world, Thou blasphemest; because I said, I am the Son of God?" (John 10:34-36). In citing "I said, ye are gods" (Psalms 82:6), Christ refers to the adjudicators of the Law, that is, the Sanhedrin ("unto whom the word of God came"), who are by Torah (Exodus 22:28) so designated. This Torah authority Jesus did not, would not, dispute, once again vindicating Himself as most lawful. Instead, he declared His own right and privilege to exposit the Law. However, by identifying Himself as one of many *elohim*[12], Christ made Himself not unique in this respect, negating deification here.

It might be argued that Christ used "elohim" to deify Himself while simultaneously using that word to publicly embarrass and deflate the Pharisees as "false gods." This, however, is only conjecture, and causes one to wonder if Jesus actually was guilty for blasphemy.

But if the argument is that a Jew is not permitted to equate Himself with one of the adjudicators of the Law, such is elitism, which was Christ's main (and not unlawful) complaint against the Pharisees.

Summation of Section

Whether Christ, Torah, or Pharisee, no "Son of God" is deified, but all these sons of God are specially authorized to speak for God and exert great influence over God's people. God, however, remains "separate" from all.

---

[11] "Thou, being a man, makest thyself God" (John 10:33).

[12] The Hebrew word "elohim" has several meanings, including God, judges of Israel, and false gods.

2. Repentance

Jesus implored the gospel of repentance among His people (Matthew 4:17). Now, if anyone pleads another to do something because it is "right" morally but does not do that thing also, we say that person is a hypocrite. The question is, did Jesus ever repent, or should He be considered a hypocrite? The Gospels are strangely silent on this critical issue, for Christ is never heard to be apologetic or seeking forgiveness.

If Jesus *did* repent, this satisfies that He was no hypocrite. Nevertheless, such repentance would denote that Jesus had sinned. Why else does anyone repent? And if Christ was not sinless, it would seem impossible that anyone should think Jesus to be God. Even that God repented, as by grieving (Genesis 6:6) or by reconsidering His actions (Exodus 32:14), does not attribute deity to Christ because *He* grieved (John 11:35) or reconsidered His actions (Matthew 26:39). For if Christ is God because they both have repented, we should attribute deity to *all* who repent, but this is impossible. Christ’s repentance would also make Him subordinate to God, for repentance must be made in front of God.

If, on the other hand, Jesus did *not* repent, He would seem to be a hypocrite, and in two ways: (1) by *saying* to repent and not *doing* repentance, and (2) by being a hypocrite while simultaneously admonishing others for being a hypocrite (the ultimate hypocrisy).

Therefore, unless we believe that the apostles were able to observe an unrepentant Jesus without thinking Him a hypocrite on the same level as those He called hypocrites, we must believe that Christ repented, and with sincerity. But whether Christ repented (the sensible conclusion) or not (which ends in hypocrisy), Christ's deification seems either way defeated by fallibility.

3. Prayer

Since praying is seeking help from or honoring one greater or more powerful, one who prays is certainly subordinate to (lesser than) the one to whom prayer is made. Christ made prayer a cornerstone of His doctrine (Matthew 6:5-15), and He prayed often (John chapter 17, Matthew 26:36-44, et al) to the Father. By this subordination, Jesus disallowed His deification.

The Trinitarian doctrine cannot produce a strong argument against this logic, and in fact makes the case worse for itself. For if the Son is equal in every way with the Father (eternal, omniscient, omnipresent, omnipotent, and immutable), it means that infinite Almighty God (the Son) prayed to infinite Almighty God (the Father). This poses unending dilemmas. Who prayed to whom? Why should God pray to Himself? Who can help God? If the explanation is that Christ possessed a dual nature ("fully God and fully man"), this simply makes it twice unresolved. That Jesus prayed to God is sensible only if Jesus is not God.

4. Conclusion

The obstacles discovered by examination of con circumstantial evidence are too many to overcome. By these results, Christ cannot be deified.

CIRCUMSTANTIAL EVIDENCE: CONCLUSION

Our goal in examining the pro and con circumstantial evidence for the deification of Christ was simply to find the Truth. Given the many obstacles uncovered, Christ cannot be deified by circumstantial evidence.

CONFESSIONAL EVIDENCE

CONFESSIONAL EVIDENCE: INTRODUCTION

Confessional evidence, like circumstantial evidence, falls under two headings, pro and con, and our goals remain the same (see Circumstantial Evidence: Introduction).

CONFESSIONAL EVIDENCE: PRO

The following pro confessional evidence will be examined in relation to the deification of Christ:

(1) "Before Abraham was, I Am."

(2) "I am the Way, the Truth, and the Life."

(3) "I am the Living Bread which came down from heaven."

(4) "Who do you say I am?"

(5) "The Father, The Son, and the Holy Spirit."

(6) "I and my Father are One."

We have chosen these sayings of Christ for their representative value in Christian doctrine. Other confessional evidence is obviously available, but this sampling covers a fair percentage of common citations in favor of Christ's deity.

1. "Verily, verily, I say unto you, Before Abraham was, *I am.*"

(John 8:58)

When Moses approached the burning bush and spoke with God concerning the release of the Hebrews from the bondage of Egypt (Exodus chapter 3), Moses asked God, "Behold, when I come to the children of Israel, and shall say unto them: The God of your fathers hath sent me unto you; and they shall say to me, What is his name? what shall

I say unto them?" (3:13). God answered, "I Am that I Am... thus shalt thou say to the children of Israel, I Am hath sent me unto you" (3:14). God's reply was not cryptic nor furtive, but honest. It was the infinite and immortal being attempting to explain the infinite and immortal to the finite and mortal.

The Christian argument is that Christ's "I am" mirrors God's "I Am." In other words, Jesus proclaimed Himself to be God. There is, however, an alternate interpretation which is the more plausible explanation. Since Christ and Torah are closely linked (as previously explicated), the statement "Before Abraham was, I am" can (and, in actuality, should) be read "Before Abraham was, Torah was." By this alternate interpretation, Christ's meaning becomes clear and twofold: **(1)** Torah (the creator of the universe, not the tablets given to Moses) chronologically came before Abraham, and **(2)** more to the point, Torah (the Law of God) takes a higher *priority* than the genetic blessing accorded to Abraham. That is, Torah comes in *importance* before Abraham. If a Jew believes his genetic affiliation to Abraham, his Jewish-ness by birth, to be his "foot in the door" to eternal life, even without his obedience to or repentance for sins committed against Torah, that Jew is in error. For although God will save a lost sheep for His name's sake (Psalms 31:3), or the entire nation of Israel for His own glory despite all of their sins (Psalms 79:8-10, Isaiah 48:8-11, Jeremiah chapter 14, et al), God still requires, "If ye seek him, he will be found of you; but if you forsake him, he will forsake you" (2 Chronicles 15:2). That is, "If they shall confess their iniquity, and the iniquity of their fathers, with their trespass which they trespassed against me, and that also they have walked contrary to me; and that I also have walked contrary unto them, and have brought them into the land of their enemies; if then their uncircumcised hearts be humbled and they then accept of the punishment of their iniquity: *then will I remember my covenant with Jacob, and with Isaac, and also my covenant with Abraham will I remember*" (Leviticus 26:40-42, italics added). Simply and explicitly, relationship to Abraham is beneficial only if one values relationship with Torah and God more so. Before Abraham comes *God and Torah*.

Jesus was thus *pleading* with certain lost sheep, those Jews who would wrap themselves in ethnicity rather than in righteousness, to avoid such arrogance of entitlement. Or, put another way, because the promise given to Father Abraham is not a bailout, no Jew should expect salvation in return for failure to repent. The same applies equally to Christians who would rely upon anything but repentance to rescue them from sin. For if a Jew by genetics (one of the chosen people) is not exempt from God's justice, a Christian by pedigree is likewise not exempt (Romans 11:17-21). Any other expectation is arrogance, which God hates (Psalms 101:5, Proverbs 8:13, et al).

2. "I am the Way, the Truth, and the Life; no one comes to the Father but by me."

(John 14:6).

This verse is easily understood. Christ is Torah, which is the Way, the Truth, and the Life. No one comes to the Father but by Torah, for the only Way *is* Torah, and the only Truth is *from* Torah, and the only Life is *in* Torah, and no man will enter into God's kingdom without obedience to and repentance for the sins committed against Torah. Christ concurs, saying that adherence to the commandments of God provides access to the Tree of Life and entry into the city of God (Revelation 22:14).

Of great relevance in the verse is the continued separation which Jesus puts between Himself and the Father. Though He and God are of one mind, Jesus in no way interchanges Himself with God. Instead, there is an understanding that Christ serves a specific purpose.

3. "I am the Living Bread which came down from heaven."

(John 6:51).

During their long travail towards the Promised Land, the Hebrews were sustained by a bread from heaven called manna (Exodus 16:4). However, Torah and Christ agree that *spiritual* sustenance is also necessary, for "Man does not live by bread alone but by every word which proceedeth out of the mouth of God" (Deuteronomy 8:3, Matthew 4:4). And what is the word which proceeds from God's mouth? Torah. Is Christ therefore manna (the physical bread) or Torah (the spiritual bread)? We believe He is the latter, the Word made flesh, Torah incarnate. Nevertheless, though He bestows upon Himself this highest honor, no self-deification is implied.

4. "Who do you say I am?"

(Matthew 16:15)

Christ's apostles all believed Him to be the Son of God (Matthew 16:16, John 6:69 & 11:27), but there is no implied deification in this, for the apostles were all Jews, ostensibly working under both an Hebraic mindset and a fear of the Sanhedrin. Supposing, however, the apostles did believe Christ to be deified, should their belief cause us to be similarly swayed? If so, why? Who were the apostles? Certainly, men chosen by Jesus, but still men with the ability to be mistaken. Are they unimpeachable simply for their proximity to Him? Let us examine this more closely, employing two instances in which an apostle appears to have deified Christ: **(1)** In the presence of a resurrected Jesus Christ, Thomas exclaimed, "My Lord and My God!" (John 20:28). Was this outburst an affirmation of Christ's deity? Or, was Thomas praising God for Christ's return? Or, was Thomas responding in awe after thrusting his hand into the side of Jesus (20:27)? In any case, Jesus does not appear to accept or even acknowledge any perceived deification from Thomas, instead speaking only of His resurrection (20:29), saying "blessed are those who have not seen" (Christ's resurrection) and "yet have believed" (in resurrection). Other interpretations are possible, but are of weaker doctrine. **(2)** John wrote, "Therefore the Jews sought the more to kill him, because he not only had broken the Sabbath, but also said that God was his father, making himself equal with God" (John 5:18). First, it is impossible to believe that Christ would break the Sabbath, for Jesus stated unequivocally that He came not to destroy the Law (Matthew 5:17). But, if He did intentionally break the Sabbath commandment, would this not have disillusioned, even repelled, Christ's apostles, all God-fearing Jews? Would not the Sanhedrin have prosecuted rightly on this basis? Would not Christian doctrine be confused if Christ (considered perfect) had broken even one commandment? Would this not destroy the idea that Christ was a sinless sacrifice? If the argument is that Jesus as God can do as He likes, this makes Christ a hypocrite (telling others to obey while he flouts the Law), unfit to be a sinless sacrifice, let alone God. Second, that "the Jews" (and perhaps even John) believed Christ had put Himself at the level of God does not signify that Jesus thought any such thing. *They* believed that He believed that He was God, but this opinion of an angry mob, the product of their imagination whipped to frenzy by their opposition to Christ (repeated in John 10:33), was meant not to elevate but to condemn Him!

In actuality, *no opinion* can deify Christ. Only Jesus is able to shed light on His own reputed godhood, but factually speaking His highest claim has been to refer to Himself as "Son of God" (John 9:35-37).

5. "Therefore go and make disciples of all nations, baptizing them in the name of the Father and of the Son and of the Holy Spirit."

(Matthew 28:19)

The meaning of the text is challenging. Disregarding for now the first part of the command (which establishes how and of whom to make disciples), and focusing on the subject of Christ's deification, can we say with certainty that “of the Father, of the Son, and of the Holy Spirit” establishes a divine triad?

Our first opposition to this doctrine of "triune God" involves that we may alternately translate the three names "Father, Son, and Holy Spirit" as "God, Torah, and Wisdom," which expresses not a Trinity of Christian doctrine but instead explains three salient and relevant concepts: (1) one God, (2) one creative force and guiding light of God (Torah), and (3) one towering hope of God for mankind (read Proverbs, chapters 1-4). With such an alternate interpretation, Christ commanded the apostles to baptize "all nations" in the name of monotheism (one God), moral righteousness (one Law), and godly intelligence (one Wisdom), all Hebraic concepts. This should startle those who think that Christ established any unauthorized precepts for His Jewish apostles or His intended Jewish audience.

It might be questioned why Christ spoke in a “code language” to His apostles rather than speaking plainly. Certainly, the Gospels illustrate a Christ who generally communicated well above the understanding of His apostles, being obligated it seems to continually explain His meanings and purposes, and frustrated that His followers were immersed in doctrine or in their own ignorance. I think we must therefore agree that His use of allegory, parable, and prophetic speech was not only intentional but also necessary to His mission. For if Jesus had been granted freedom to communicate simply, He would have done so.

The key to deciphering Jesus is the Hebraic mindset, which must be applied in every instance. With the Hebraic mindset, the words of Christ (a Jew, learned and speaking of the highest Jewish ideas and ideals) are illuminated correctly. Without this key, a huge problem, both in volume and consequence, follows. Jesus (quoting Isaiah) echoed these thoughts, saying that those who have not been given the “eyes” and the “ears” shall not understand, nor be converted, nor healed (Matthew 13:16). Use the Hebraic mindset, He hinted, and "Go not into the way of the Gentiles" (Matthew 10:5). Thus, if "Father, Son, and Holy Spirit" have become confused with a triune god, it is no fault of Christ for any so-called carelessness in using cryptic phrases, but the fault of men who make misinterpretations while seeking to divine the truth.

Our second opposition to this doctrine of Trinity is based upon the first opposition, that those who see Christ as establishing a Trinity do so by disregarding Christ's Jewish background, Jewish goals, Jewish apostles, Jewish audience, and Hebraic mindset. For if Christ had ever deviated from that which is Torah, His Jewish followers would have abandoned Him promptly, not tempting the wrath of God nor upsetting the Pharisees for the sake of half-baked theories or questionable righteousness. But if one believes that Christ's Jewish followers were of some different stripe than other Jews, this fails to account for the thousands of Jewish Christians who also were zealous for the Law (Acts 21:20), who would have immediately left Christ if He or any of His apostles were not righteous by Torah. Saying otherwise is a great suspension of disbelief.

It might be argued that Christ did not *establish* Trinity, but that Trinity is and has always been an Hebraic concept. The evidence for this argument is that in Torah (Genesis 1:2, 1:26, 3:22, et al) God seems to speak of His multiplicity. However, such evidence has alternate interpretations. When God, for example, says "Let *us*..." (Genesis 1:26), it may be inferred that He is speaking to angels and not to another "aspect" of Himself, a strong counter-argument.

A weaker Christian argument is that Christ, on the road to Emmaus, "expounded unto them in all the scriptures the things concerning himself" (Luke 24:27). But this verse is unclear, teaching no concepts of Trinity per se, any doctrine gained being only through interpolation.

In fact, Trinity is a *departure* from Torah and Tanakh, for "Hear, O Israel: The Lord our God is one Lord" (Deuteronomy 6:4), "Thou shalt have no other gods before me" (Deuteronomy 5:7), and "Thus saith the Lord the King of Israel and his redeemer the Lord of hosts: I am the first and I am the last; and beside me there is no God" (Isaiah 44:6).

Our third opposition to the Trinitarian doctrine is based upon the second opposition, that only by creative Gentile license has Trinity been established. Not until the Nicene (325/381 AD) and Athanasian (circa 500 AD) creeds were enshrined did Trinity become a church-wide doctrine. Furthermore, many non-Jewish Christians in those times were opposed to a triune God, and the creeds did not claim victory without much denominational battling, some quite violent. Even to this day, not all Christian denominations follow the Trinitarian formula, but some deviate slightly from "homoousios" (e.g., United Pentecostal Church), some totally reject doctrinal tests of faith (e.g., Quakers), some say that belief in Trinity is not required for salvation (e.g., Church of Christ), and some (Unitarians, Christadelphians, Jehovah's Witnesses) place Christ at a level altogether different from (lower than) God[13].

It might be argued that Trinitarian doctrine is not the result of denominational superiority but was understood by the earliest Christian theologians. For example, 1 John Chapter 5 would seem to uphold Trinity. However, this supposition is incorrect in at least two ways, John asserting that: **(1)** the three (Father, Word, and Holy Ghost) are "one" not by a Trinitarian nature or by their inseparable deity, but by simple agreement regarding their witness (this point specifically and repeatedly stressed), and **(2)** the Father, the Word, and the Holy Ghost are witnesses to Christ, the Word made flesh, indicating that Christ is actually *fourth,* bursting the entire Trinitarian formula. Further, the three witness the

---

[13] And the further these denominations vary from Trinitarian doctrine, the more the established Christian hierarchy seems to marginalize or reject them.

fourth (Christ) from heaven (and other places), signifying that Christ is separate. The rest of John's message (to verse 13) concerns obedience to commandments, and belief in eternal life through Torah. In sum, 1 John 5 not only weakens the Trinitarian doctrine, but gives strength to the Hebraic mindset.

Our fourth opposition to the Trinitarian doctrine derives from Christ's own estimations of Himself in relation to both the Father and the Holy Spirit.

In comparison to God, the Father, Jesus said, "Why callest thou me good? there is none good but one, that is, God" (Mark 10:18). Two propositions arise from this. The first proposition is that Jesus is God ("one"), and that Christ was hinting or even demanding that He be deified. That is, "If you call me good, you should be prepared to call me God." This proposition is not only pure inference but also rash speculation, for it indicates a very manipulative and quite alien Christ. The second proposition is that Jesus is *not* God, and that He was deflecting any undue glorification. That is, "I'm not God, so stop calling me good." This proposition is more sensible, Christ rejecting the notion that He should be elevated to the status "good," that is, God. Whatever the mood or the cause, Christ drew a distinction between the goodness of God and the goodness of everyone else, including Himself. Jesus would not allow Himself to be equated with God, but actually doubted the relationship of God's goodness to His goodness, an existential moment. Thus, by His own doubts, Jesus declared God to be "most good," that is, "more good" than Christ. Christ is therefore unequal with and separate from God, that is, not God. It might be argued that the human form of God (Son) is lesser than the divine form (Father), but this argument is desperation, grasping at straws in order to salvage incorrect doctrine. Can God be imperfectly human ("less good") and yet still be God ("most good")? This is not logical.

In comparison to the Holy Spirit, Jesus says, "Whosoever speaketh a word against the Son of man, it shall be forgiven him: but whosoever speaketh against the Holy Ghost, it shall not be forgiven him, neither in this world, neither in the world to come" (Matthew 12:32). The cornerstone here is whether we allow "Son of man" to mean Christ. If so, Christ has indicated that the Holy Spirit (Ghost) must be for one's own spiritual security treated more reverentially than the Son of God. The reason is not clear for the more stringent punishment for blasphemy against the different spiritual parties[14], but there is in any case found an inequality between Son and Holy Spirit, which conclusion rejects again the Trinitarian doctrine.

Since Christ Himself spoke of major differences between Father, Son, and Holy Spirit, the Trinitarian doctrine does not stand. In sum, Christ cannot be deified by the doctrine of Trinity.

6. "I and my Father are one."

(John 10:30)

The Word and God ("I and my Father") are not one in the physical sense. As already examined, **(1)** Christ died but God cannot die, and **(2)** Christ and God are not one as in Trinitarian doctrine. Instead, Christ and God are one in *mind,* as on the same wavelength, that is, identically desiring certain behaviors from the Jewish people, expecting certain improvements from the Pharisees, and upholding the same Law of God. When the Word (Christ) transmits the desires of God, they are indeed *one* for that common transmission. Their message is the same, therefore they are one. As a recording transmits only what is recorded, Christ (the recording) transmitted only that which God desired to transmit. For, "I

[14] Perhaps the Holy Spirit is of a more sensitive nature than the Son, or the Father is more protective of the Holy Spirit than of the Son.

must be about my Father's business" (Luke 2:49), "My doctrine is not mine but his that sent me" (John 7:16), and "If ye had known me, ye should have known my Father also" (John 8:19). This is the loyalty of the Word, not the deity of Christ.

7. Conclusion

The obstacles discovered by examination of pro confessional evidence are too many to overcome, and also there are sufficient alternate plausible interpretations and explanations. By these results, Christ cannot be deified.

CONFESSIONAL EVIDENCE: CON

Con confessional evidence will be examined under two subheadings which seem most suitable for this subject: (1) position, and (2) anguish.

1. Position

Jesus often made statements which revealed His true place in the celestial hierarchy. These include:

(1) "I can of mine own self do nothing" (John 5:30), exhibiting helplessness.

(2) "I seek not mine own will, but the will of the Father which sent me" (John 5:30), exhibiting that Christ has a will of His own which is different than God's, surrendered for the mission of Christ.

(3) "If I bear witness of myself, my witness is not true" (John 5:31), exhibiting humility and lack of ultimate authority.

(4) "Do not think that I will accuse you to the Father" (John 5:45), exhibiting a separateness from God, *even in the spirit realm.*

These confessional remarks (and many more like them) display a Jesus who clearly knew His role and limitations, subordinate to (lower than) God. This is obviously an obstacle to faith in Christ's deity.

2. Anguish

At Gethsemane, Jesus beseeched the Lord God, "Remove this cup from me," and sweated blood for the pressure He felt concerning His upcoming crucifixion (Luke 22:42). Clearly, these were moments of faltering for Christ, of anxiety in front of God, and subordination (finally) to the will of God.

More harrowing was Christ at Calvary, crying, "My God, My God, why hast thou forsaken me?" (Matthew 27:46). Here, the Son was not only in anguish but also believed Himself separated from the Father, thereby negating homoousios, which demands a constant and everlasting togetherness.

Christ's torments thus provide considerable obstacles to faith in His deity.

3. Conclusion

Our examination of con confessional evidence produced a verdict of no deification.

CONFESSIONAL EVIDENCE: CONCLUSION

Our goal in examining the pro and con confessional evidence for the deification of Christ was again simply to find the Truth. Given the many obstacles uncovered, Christ cannot be deified by confessional evidence.

GENERAL CONCLUSIONS

Both circumstantial and confessional evidence failed to verify Christ's deity. In some cases, doctrine could not withstand logical conclusion. In other cases, doctrine did not account for contradictory evidence from the Gospels and/or Torah. We therefore do not believe Jesus Christ to be deified, and furthermore think the Christian doctrine of Trinity to be a false doctrine.

We nevertheless believe from the evidence examined that Jesus was an extraordinary figure in history, given much power, wisdom, and influence by God for a specific purpose. He is worthy of honor for His gifts and talents; and worthy of praise for His honesty, loyalty, courage, determination, fortitude, compassion, outreach, and the many other superior qualities which He displayed.

Jesus Christ was not, however, just a great man or a great prophet. We believe Him to have been a true representative of God, in fact, the Son of God, that is, Torah personified. This cannot, however, elevate Him beyond the position warranted by the evidence of the Gospels, Torah, and logic. Simply, we do not deify the Son of God.

AFTERWORD

We continue to refer to Christ as He and Him, with a capital H, not for deification purposes, nor even for courtesy towards Christian doctrines, but for reverential feelings towards Him as the Son of God, that is, as Torah personified. Although some might disagree with such use of capitalization, we believe this transmits proper respect, in the same manner that respectful Jews capitalize the S in Sages.

The Hebraic Mindset is Essential

by Tom Wise

INTRODUCTION

If one means to read the Bible with any true understanding, it must be with an Hebraic mindset. It cannot be otherwise. Every bit of Tanakh (Old Testament) is Hebraic. The Gospels are Hebraic. Jesus Christ is Hebraic. Even those commentaries of New Testament not often thought to be Hebraic are to great degree.

For our purposes, "Hebraic" means one thing, which is "of or from Torah (the Law of God)." Having an Hebraic mindset is therefore employing this correct lens when seeing or hearing any particular thing. It is asking oneself, "Is what I am seeing or hearing of or from Torah?" In terms of dividing truth from fiction, having an Hebraic mindset is determining through Torah whether the words and deeds of any person, or the maxims of any doctrine, are correct or incorrect.

The Hebraic mindset differs from a "Jewish mindset" in that a Jewish mindset may include additional cultural, ethnic, and/or doctrinal information which dilutes the importance of Torah. Most often, however, the acquired Jewish mindset and the mandatory (Torah) Hebraic mindset overlap. This gives the Jewish mind (except where secularism has encroached) an advantage over others. On this point, that the Jew has such advantage, Paul agrees (Romans 3:1-2).

While the Hebraic mindset is rooted in Torah, and most often transmitted through Jews (or Hebrews), the intended audience is not necessarily Jewish, but includes also the non-Jew, that is, the Gentile, who is open to Torah conversion. Under the administration of Christ's Jewish apostles, the Christian church first operated in this manner, disallowing any who would not convert to Torah. At some point, however, there came a dispute over whether non-Jews should be so converted (Acts 15:1-5), leading to a puzzling compromise of Torah obedience for non-Jewish Christians, that is, four minimum standards with an additional hope for future Hebraic mindset (15:20-21). This split widened in a further "understanding" that Jewish Christians would adhere to Torah in its entirety but non-Jewish Christians would have no such obligation (Acts 21:15-26). In hostility, Paul brought this to a boiling point, railing against all manner of Hebraic mindset, whether Jewish or non-Jewish (Book of Galatians). Despite Paul's later backtracking (Book of Romans), the transmittal of Hebraic mindset to non-Jews, especially to non-Jewish Christians, was thereafter derogated as evangelistic "Judaizing." In centuries to follow, this became within Christian regions a punishable (and often capital) offense.

Ironically, the Christian aversion to Hebraic mindset rejects the Hebraic mindset of Jesus Christ. Not only did Christ adhere to an Hebraic mindset for determining between righteous and unrighteous, but also He commissioned his disciples to Judaize the world (Matthew 28:19-20)[15]! Will anyone say that Jesus desired some different method of determination, or some different form of religion? Is it of the heart? That organ is weakness. Is it of the mind? That is the playground of deceit. Is it of some different Law? We know this to be untrue. For Christ, and therefore Christians, it is the Hebraic mindset which is essential.

1. The Argument for Torah

All Scripture is or must be based on Torah. For the Jew this is not controversial, but for any other there is likely to be a question, if not conflict. The Christian, however, should not balk, for it is plain that Christ studied, taught, and utilized Torah; that He commanded His disciples to follow Torah and to obey the administrators of Torah (the Sanhedrin); that He predicated eternal life and access to Paradise on

[15] Though He at first had no inclination to go to Gentiles or Samaritans (Matthew 10:5-6).

obedience to Torah; and that He labeled anyone who taught otherwise to be "least." The Muslim should likewise understand that Islamic Law has its basis in Torah (some 2500 years its elder), despite how much more aggressive are Islamic courts of justice.

Torah is not only foundational to the monotheistic religions but has every right to claim itself as the basis for much or all current morality (including its antitheses). For example, English common law, especially in its organization of government, was almost certainly founded upon Torah[16]. That system, though modified by monarchy through the centuries, became the foundation again for the American Constitution and its representative republic. As another example, it has been theorized that Native American Indians are in whole or in part descended from the Jews, their governance and moral law quite like Torah. Certain artifacts, such as the Decalogue boulder (located near Los Lunas, New Mexico), and stones hewn with Hebrew inscriptions (found in 1860 near Newark, Ohio), add to that thrust. Other such surprising connections exist, including between the Jewish people and the Japanese people, and between Buddha and Jesus Christ!

2. Torah Universal

While religions differ on commandment and rite, all individuals, even those who claim no religion, adhere to one morality. Specifically, though a man may believe, through all manner of religious constructs and codes of ethics, that his own stealing is above reproach and retribution, that same man will be enraged if something is stolen from him. This is where the buck always stops. True morality, therefore, not based on hypocrisy but on truth, embodies itself in the Golden Rule, that is, "Love thy neighbor as thyself." In other words, true morality is the reciprocity of conduct, to treat others as you would like to be treated.

This code of conduct is not, however, subjective. Three basic tenets must be always addressed and respected: (1) Life, (2) Liberty, and (3) Private Property. That is, no man desires his life to be unwillingly taken, his

[16] It has been expounded that the Anglo-Saxons were perhaps descendants of Joseph's sons, Ephraim and Manasseh.

freedom to be fraudulently impinged, or the work of his hands to be involuntarily taken. This is ironclad, and the reciprocity of it comprises true morality.

Torah is the protector of, and arguably the original design for, this true morality. Torah covers it fully, and provides through the Ten Commandments the briefest yet clearest synopsis.

Besides this reciprocity between men, Torah also explains man's entire duty to God. In so doing, men are freed from exploitation by more oppressive religions. For where Torah ends, tyranny begins.

Torah not only provides regulation through Law, but also properly delineates all jurisprudence. Such concepts as (1) "innocent until proven guilty," (2) witnesses, and (3) fair judgment based on impartiality are all of Torah origination. Not only are these, but the concepts of mercy and grace are also from and within Torah.

Therefore, all men agreeing mercy to be the godliest attribute, and freedom in reciprocity to be the correct state of man's being, Torah must be recognized as superior to all other documents of morality (even those derived from it).

3. The Essential Hebraic Mindset

Since Torah is foundational and the fountain of all good[17], it is imperative that we understand it correctly. In this arena, the legitimate qualification of the Jew cannot be overstated (especially since the language of Torah is Hebrew).

Christians may bristle, but their Savior is a Torah Jew, that is, Jesus, who commanded obedience to Torah (see "The Arrogance"). In fact, Christianity began as a path for Gentiles to become Torah Jews. And though Paul at first attempted to disconnect Jewish ways from the rest of Christianity, he later wrote that the Jews were uniquely enabled by God

[17] Naturally, God is the fountain, but Torah (like Jesus Christ) is God's Word in temporal form.

to provide guidance in righteousness, as the oracles of it (Romans 3:1-2). It is therefore astounding that any Christian should not desire the Hebraic mindset.

Islam also should not claim a different avenue. Ishmael, Islam's traditional first, was brother to Isaac. True, he received his own blessing, but Ishmael will always be a "wild man" (Genesis 16:12), hardly an endorsement for the role of fair judge. That Islam has taken the blind path away from Torah towards needless bloodshed and tyrannical oppression evidences that nature, and proves the Hebraic mindset worthier and necessary.

Arguments abound. Some will retain a notion that a mindset different than Hebraic is superior. Others will oppose it on principle (such as, "Correct and proper interpretation is relative to one's experience and knowledge"). Many will merely scoff. Naturally, my conclusions are cause for upset. This is understandable, for all wish to be respected and none to feel inferior. However, correct and proper interpretation of the scriptures is not a matter of feelings or etiquette, but of accuracy and logic. For the scriptures are not merely morality plays meant to direct one's individual desires towards personal growth, but also are delineation of boundaries which have no flexibility beyond parameters which are already settled. Put another way, scripture is not only self-help, it is also commanded behavior. Such things must therefore be viewed with exactitude, and the Hebraic mindset is the precise lens.

4. Who's in Charge?

Why the Jew? Besides his antecedence to the Christian and Muslim, the Jew has been chosen by God. Abraham, the first Hebrew, was selected as the father of all three great monotheistic religions. Moses, a Hebrew, was made the lawgiver. Isaiah, a Jew, was the great prophet to the world. Jesus Christ, a Jew.

From the beginning, the Jew has been persistent to survive through every type of slavery and persecution, has vigorously defended his own heritage and ethnicity, and has meticulously preserved Torah in its current state for at least 2500 years[18].

It therefore seems clear that the Jew is especially suited and elected for the position of oracle.

5. The Hebraic Mindset Explained

The lens of the Hebraic mindset determines whether any action or any word is of or from Torah. This is accomplished not by whim but by proper jurisprudence, as previously explained. The method used is comparison of action or word against Torah parameter.

Who is permitted to judge between right and wrong? While Sages and scholars, especially through Talmud, have long been respected for their counsel, all who purpose to use the Hebraic mindset are qualified to so discern, and there is no Torah barrier which disallows this. However, excepting for those commandments which explicitly state otherwise, only the adjudicators of the Law (Sanhedrin) have the authority to administer punishments for transgressions against Torah Law. The Hebraic mindset does not permit vigilantism (the concept of "Zealot" notwithstanding).

The non-Jew often ignores this Jewish authority and proper Hebraic mindset. It is in fact commonly-held doctrine, especially among Christians, that the power of Torah ought to be dismissed entirely. According to this doctrine, the punishments for sin against God's commandments have been overthrown by the crucifixion of Christ. This, however, refutes Christ's own teachings. Further, it flies in the face of reason, for how shall one reject Torah and yet embrace the Ten Commandments, the core of Torah?

What is the limit of interpretation? First, any interpretation clearly against Torah is impermissible. There is, for example, no interpolation which makes adultery righteous. Second, there has for some millennia been a "battle" between the literalist (Sadducee) and the far-reaching exegetic (Pharisee). In Christ's time, for example, the Pharisees believed ~~in bodily resurrection but the~~ Sadducees did not (Mark 12:18). Third, it is

[18] Scholars believe that when Ezra rediscovered the Book of the Law, certain small changes were made. Thereafter, it retained its integrity.

within the Hebraic mindset that more than one correct answer may apply to any particular question of righteousness. The vagueness of particular commandments permits this on one hand, the harshness of certain punishments for transgressions demands the mercy of the Law on the other.

A common complaint against Torah (and religious law in general) is that some of its commandments seem archaic, that is, outdated. This complaint, however, is only a front for the true motive, which is to remove Torah from blocking the way against one or another forbidden human desire. There is, for example, no doubt that Torah forbids homosexuality, and those who prefer or sympathize with this sexual practice call such commandment "intolerant" and "ignorant," saying also that the Hebraic mindset is "bigoted." How so? First, the homosexuality forbidden is male, not female. This is targeted. Second, it is the sexual act, not the proclivity (for example, being "born gay"), which is punishable. This is specific. In the same manner, an angry disposition is not punished until a forbidden violent act is committed. Third, there must be two, if not three, witnesses to the sexual act in order to render a verdict of guilt. This is merciful.

The Hebraic mindset does not work according to emotional reaction. Judgment and punishment are rendered on purely legal grounds. As well, the adjudicators are forbidden to judge with respect to any person's income or power. All is fair. Nevertheless, there is mercy in the law, and every effort is made to find innocence, not guilt. And certainly, it is not incorrect or forbidden to have compassion for any sinner. This mercy and compassion does not, however, translate into moderation of lawful application, for that is moral relativity, impermissible. Neither is peaceful tolerance within the community a reason to mollify or recede from Torah. In sum, commandments are not recognized as valuable for satisfying the desires of every person. Not only is such not possible, but also the desire to satisfy sinful desires signifies an arrogance against God. One either accepts Torah fully or one does not. This is the Hebraic mindset.

Some commandments seem to serve no purpose at all. The ordinance to refrain from a garment comprised of both wool and linen appears to be one such, a commandment of ancient mystery[19]. Nevertheless, because it is Torah, it cannot be waved off without consequences. We ignore it at our own peril. This is the Hebraic mindset.

Is it then an Hebraic mindset to obey blindly? Hardly. First, we know that God's wish is obedience through love, for He tells us to "love the Lord thy God with all thy heart, and all thy soul, and all thy might" (Deuteronomy 6:5). In other words, we obey because we believe that God and His commandments are good. Second, if the love of and/or faith in God or His commandments is momentarily absent, obedience (respect) through fear is quite proper, for "the fear of the Lord is the beginning of wisdom" (Proverbs 9:10). This aspect is quite complicated but perfectly practicable and acceptable to Him. Third, the road to the Hebraic mindset is well-forged. For millennia, Jews have questioned what this or that commandment means, and the oracles (the prophets and the Sages) have provided illumination, much of it published. Not that every possible avenue has been traversed, but the existing body of Hebraic exposition is vast.

The goal of Torah, and therefore of the Hebraic mindset, is maximum freedom, with the free will nevertheless exercised within the confines of true morality.

6. The Christian Mindset

Christ did not "fulfill" Torah by dying on the cross. He fulfilled it by being perfect in the Law, evidenced by the Sanhedrin's inability to find guilt in Him without false witnesses (and other incorrect jurisprudence). The Christian who therefore obeys Torah is quite correct, despite doctrine to the contrary. To follow Christ is to be a Torah Jew.

But if Christ did fulfill the Law in the Christian doctrinal sense, there is no need to fear disobedience even against the Ten Commandments. Such is logical. Nevertheless, no Christian believer would agree to it, and, furthermore, the church still expects voluntary compliance to this "moral

[19] It is likely a commandment of separation, to distinguish between the believer and non-believer. Certainly, it is culture-specific, but no less vital to God.

law," as well to as other commandments of specific import (for example, tithing and bans on sexual conduct)[20]. In other words, the Christian is not free from the Law of God, nor does he behave so. Christian doctrine against the power of Torah has therefore failed.

7. New Testament Proof of Hebraic Mindset

"And the brethren immediately sent away Paul and Silas by night unto Berea; who coming thither went into the synagogue of the Jews. These were more noble than those in Thessalonica, in that they received the word with all readiness of mind, and searched the scriptures daily, whether those things were so. Therefore, many of them believe."

(Acts 17:10-12)

In order to discern whether or not "the word" they received from Paul and Silas was or was not righteous, the Berean Jews searched daily through "the scriptures," that is, through the Law (especially) and the Prophets[21]. This is the Hebraic mindset in action.

The Berean Jews were elevated for their diligent research (and for their "readiness of mind"), being called "more noble." It might be argued that such nobility was bestowed on them for having "received the word" or because "many of them believe." Perhaps, but it cannot be denied that their Hebraic mindset brought them to such conclusion.

---

[20] It is a further weakness of Christian doctrine that it mandates one portion of Torah (the "moral law"), but disregards, except when convenient, other portions (for example, the "Levitical law"), yet simultaneously makes the case that every man is a sinner for failing to fulfill every particle of the Law!

[21] It should be obvious that Berean Jews would have consulted only the Law and the Prophets, that is, Old Testament. But even if they had consulted any New Testament document (if any existed), none would have presumptuously labeled any such document as "scripture."

Let us examine this more closely:

(1) The Berean Jews listened intently ("with all readiness of mind") to Paul and Silas, more attuned to these outsiders than their Thessalonian brethren[22] (Acts 17:5-9). Nevertheless, the Berean Jews at this point were employing not an Hebraic mindset, only courtesy.

(2) The immediate reaction of the Berean Jews towards "the word" received was neither to weep for joy nor to gnash teeth, but instead to immerse themselves in scripture (the Law and the Prophets) to glean truth. The lesson communicated is that doctrine promoted by one of even Paul's stature is not unimpeachable. There is a *higher* source to consult. This understanding is the Hebraic mindset.

(3) The Berean Jews searched scripture not for a day, but "daily." Note several sides of the Hebraic mindset revealed here. First, their examination was deliberate. By a slow process, doctrine compared to the Law and the Prophets revealed Truth. Second, their scholarship was serious. Likely, they hotly debated this issue.

(4) Without doubt, the Berean Jews scrutinized Jesus to see if by the Law of God (Torah) He was righteous or a scoundrel. Certainly, if they thought any of the words or actions of Christ to be sinful (that is, against Torah) they would not have believed on Him.

Some might say this shows a great stubbornness of the Jews. This stubbornness, however, was integral to their being "more noble." For Acts 17:11 imparts that the greatest portion of their nobility was in, after hearing the word, searching the Word. It is thus logical to assert that if they had *not* searched the scriptures for the veracity of that which was preached to them, their nobility would have been diminished, even disappeared. Such stubbornness is thus positive, not negative[23].

[22] Berea was just a short distance from Thessalonica.

[23] The negative connotation would be that the Berean Jews were "less ignoble" than the Thessalonians, not "more noble."

(5) That the Berean Jews embraced Jesus Christ (or at least "the word" from Paul and Silas) evidences that He survived their particular Hebraic mindset "truth filter." They accepted, but not from any persuasion to abandon Torah for Christ, but rather because Christ agreed with Torah!

Supposing, however, that the Berean Jews had in the end rejected Christ, we must agree they were still "noble" for deciding through an Hebraic mindset.

8. To Search or Not to Search

In the verse from Acts, the original Greek for "searched" is *anakrino*. Strong's Concordance tells us this word in context means "to investigate, to examine closely, to judge, to interrogate, to scrutinize, to sift, to question." The Berean Jews carried this out nobly, but how many others do not? How many accept doctrine without research and judicious thought? And why?

It might be argued that there no longer is any necessity to search, to be noble, to perform an Hebraic mindset upon Jesus Christ, for such has already been conducted to satisfaction, leaving no room for disagreement or even discussion. Such an argument is astoundingly shallow and incorrect, constituting abdication of one's natural intelligence to the opinions of other men. Shamefully, there is no excuse for such laziness, for the printing press and personal computer have made available to nearly every man the Bible and other important documents.

Ignorance makes easy prey for the great deceiver. Those who refuse to "daily" search the scriptures may be misled by those who unintentionally distort the truth (leaders well-meaning but in error), or manipulated by those who intentionally lie. It is therefore imperative to understand by the power of one's own faculties. Otherwise, without discernment, especially that of the Hebraic mindset, doctrines of men creep in to distort and destroy in darkness that which was beforehand meticulously constructed in light. This is not only rhetoric but historical fact, and also of current import, for at this moment are elements and factions tearing apart from the inside our religions and churches. The average man depends upon the clergyman, but who has tested the clergyman for his nobility? And from which spring did that clergyman drink? And from whence did that spring originate?

Am I too harsh? Shall I tone it down? Many will say that I am and that I should. Amazingly, there is a widespread preference for ignorance, which preference sometimes even turns militant, those without understanding attacking any attempt to be "more noble," especially if through an Hebraic mindset. Even my observation of this phenomenon is at risk for targeting! But why should I allow the souls of many to languish? Surely it is not that we seek quantity without quality, pews filled with those rabid yet errant. How many must fall to antinomianism? To dereliction of charity? To abomination? Is it not better to have small churches populated with Hebraic (true) Christians than large edifices brimming with incorrect lemmings?

9. The Hebraic Mindset in the Church

To be frank, the Christian church has never been amenable to the Hebraic mindset. The church generally approaches scripture as if the words were written by non-Jews, or by Jews for non-Jews. Christian commentaries abound which bolster this idea, even suggesting that to come near with an Hebraic mindset is wrong, therefore often omitting that paradigm or using it even as a negative lesson.

Some Christians, however, *are* noble. They scrutinize the sermons and the lesson plans, relying not on "feelings" or "mysteries" but, as the Berean Jews, on corroboration through the Law and the Prophets. Not surprisingly, these noble face opposition from peers. For their work, they endure patronizing sighs and slander, sometimes being called "heretics" or "legalists" (this latter is actually a compliment). Frequently, they have been excommunicated, asked to remove themselves to another place. In times past, some were put to death. All this because they dared test ancient doctrine with an Hebraic mindset.

But why this Christian fear and loathing?

10. The Root of the Problem

The bias against an Hebraic mindset is, unfortunately, ancient, anti-Semitic, and intentional. Without dilution, the early "church fathers" openly stated their desire to erase Judaic thought from the Christian religion[24].

Consider this typical letter (emphasis added) from the Emperor Constantine "to all those not present at the Council of Nicea" (ca. 325 AD):

When the question relative to the sacred festival of Easter arose, it was universally thought that it would be convenient that all should keep the feast on one day; for what could be more beautiful and more desirable, than to see this festival, through which we receive the hope of immortality, celebrated by all with one accord, and in the same manner? It was declared to be particularly unworthy for this, the holiest of all festivals, to follow the custom [the calculation] of *the Jews, who had soiled their hands with the most fearful of crimes,* and whose minds were blinded. In rejecting their custom, we may transmit to our descendants the legitimate mode of celebrating Easter, which we have observed from the time of the Saviour's Passion to the present day [according to the day of the week].

We ought not, therefore, to have anything in common with the Jews, for the Saviour has shown us another way; our worship follows a more legitimate and more convenient course (the order of the days of the week); and consequently, in unanimously adopting this mode, we desire, dearest brethren, *to separate ourselves from the detestable company of the Jews,* for it is truly shameful for us to hear them boast that without their direction we could not keep this feast. How can they be in the right, they who, after the death of the Saviour, have no longer been led by reason but by wild violence, as their delusion may urge them? They do not possess the truth in this Easter question; for, in their blindness and repugnance to all improvements, they frequently celebrate two passovers in the same year. We could not imitate those who are openly in error. How, then, could we follow these Jews, who are most certainly blinded by error? for to celebrate the passover twice in one year is totally inadmissible. *But even if this were not so, it would still be your duty not to tarnish your soul by communications with such wicked people [the Jews].*

---

[24] See Ignatius, *Epistle to the Magnesians* (published ca. 98-117 AD), Justin Martyr, *Dialogue with Trypho* (published ca. 138-161 AD), Origen of Alexandria (b. 185-d. 254 AD), John Chrysostom (b. 347-d. 407 AD).

Besides, consider well, that in such an important matter, and on a subject of such great solemnity, there ought not to be any division. Our Saviour has left us only one festal day of our redemption, that is to say, of his holy passion, and he desired [to establish] only one Catholic Church. Think, then, how unseemly it is, that on the same day some should be fasting whilst others are seated at a banquet; and that after Easter, some should be rejoicing at feasts, whilst others are still observing a strict fast. For this reason, a Divine Providence wills that this custom should be rectified and regulated in a uniform way; and everyone, I hope, will agree upon this point.

As, on the one hand, *it is our duty not to have anything in common with the murderers of our Lord*; and as, on the other, the custom now followed by the Churches of the West, of the South, and of the North, and by some of those of the East, is the most acceptable, it has appeared good to all; and I have been guarantee for your consent, that you would accept it with joy, as it is followed at Rome, in Africa, in all Italy, Egypt, Spain, Gaul, Britain, Libya, in all Achaia, and in the dioceses of Asia, of Pontus, and Cilicia. You should consider not only that the number of churches in these provinces make a majority, but also that it is right to demand what our reason approves, and that *we should have nothing in common with the Jews.*

To sum up in few words: By the unanimous judgment of all, it has been decided that the most holy festival of Easter should be everywhere celebrated on one and the same day, and it is not seemly that in so holy a thing there should be any division. As this is the state of the case, accept joyfully the divine favour, and this truly divine command; for all which takes place in assemblies of the bishops ought to be regarded as proceeding from the will of God. Make known to your brethren what has been decreed, keep this most holy day according to the prescribed mode; we can thus celebrate this holy Easter day at the same time, if it is granted me, as I desire, to unite myself with you; we can rejoice together, seeing that the divine power has made use of our instrumentality for destroying the evil designs of the devil, and thus causing faith, peace, and unity to flourish amongst us. May God graciously protect you, my beloved brethren.

(Source: Eusebius, Vita Const., Lib. iii., 18-20)

As is apparent, the original scriptural religion, Judaism (and, by extension, Christ's Jewish church), was by Constantine's time deemed unsuitable for Christians. For centuries thereafter, even to the present day, a Christian who adopted an Hebraic mindset would receive at least an admonishment, and Jews in the surrounding areas would be blamed, placed in danger for that which the Book of Acts calls "noble."

11. Baseless Hatred

"Sinat hinam" is Hebrew for "baseless hatred." This is an apt term for the emotion directed from those who defend incorrect doctrines against those who prove those doctrines to be incorrect. The Hebraic mindset proves through Torah (the arbiter between correct and incorrect), and by logic, Trinitarian Christianity to be incorrect doctrine (see also "The Arrogance")[25]. Consequently, besides the aforementioned anti-Semitic and anti-Judaic attitudes, the Trinitarian has a hatred for Torah and Hebraic mindset. This hatred is baseless, however, for Torah can never be heretical.

Nevertheless, it goes deeper. Sinat hinam against the Hebraic mindset is also satanic. This is not overstatement, for to be against Torah is to be anti-Christ.

12. Anti-Christ

Jesus said that anyone who breaks the least commandment of God's Law, and teaches men so, will be called least in the kingdom of heaven, but anyone who does and teaches for the least commandment will be called great (Matthew 5:19). It must be agreed that by "commandment" Christ meant Torah commandment. Therefore, to teach against any Torah commandment is to be against Christ, to be antichrist.

Consider also that Jesus never broke Torah commandment. At every turn, the Pharisees where thwarted by the great legalism and Hebraic mindset of Christ. In order to convict Him at all, the Sanhedrin had to bring false witnesses[26], and their charge of blasphemy was applied

---

[25] Revelation, chapters 2 & 3, relates that the church consists six times from seven of an incorrect flavor, whether by error of attitude or doctrine. Close study here is recommended.

without cause. With sincerity and integrity, Jesus was never anti-Torah. Thus, to be for Christ is to be for Torah. It might be argued that Jesus was perfect in Torah in order to make Himself a sinless sacrifice, that sacrifice not only having power to remit the punishment for sins but also having efficacy to fulfill for all time the necessary obedience to the Law. However, not only is this doctrine incorrect but also it teaches Christians to break least commandments, therefore making this Christian doctrine antichrist! Supposing, however, my counter-argument not persuasive enough, note also that Jesus commanded His disciples to follow every directive from the Pharisees, only warning them to avoid hypocrisy, that is, to avoid saying and not doing (Matthew 23:2-3). Is this not promotion of Torah?

Jesus Christ neither broke nor taught against any least Torah commandment. He was never anti-Torah. But He also was pro-Torah, utilizing it at various times to justify His teachings as "works of the father" and to fight the seductions of Satan. Whoever then does not employ Torah is against the manner of Christ.

We furthermore cannot separate Christ's ethnicity, upbringing, and culture from His mission. Jesus was Jewish in every manner, and if this were not God's intention Christ would have been born as other than a Jew. To be against the Jews, that is, anti-Semitic[27] is also thus anti-Christ.

13. Gentile Christianity

To be a Gentile is to be a non-Jew, that is, to be worshipping other than the one true God. It is not a good thing to be Gentile (atheist, pagan, polytheist, and so forth). Paul, in fact, comments that a Gentile is only worthy when utilizing an Hebraic mindset, that is, when doing "the things contained in the law" (Romans 2:14) [28]. Why then is the Christian

[26] This grave sin against the Ninth Commandment proves the Sanhedrin's sinat hinam against Christ.

[27] How is it possible to have hatred for Jews yet claim to follow a *Jewish* Lord and Savior?

church against the Hebraic mindset? Why is the Christian church Gentile?

The Christian church permits pagan infiltration, from such benign elements as the Christmas tree to the very severe errors of Trinitarian idolatry and salvation by vicarious sacrifice. Even the solemn event of communion is a diluted pagan ritual. Gnostic philosophy is evident within its precepts, and borrowed sayings from mystery religions hang on like leeches. Why is this permitted? Why is the Christian church Gentile?

The first likely response from the Christian is that Jesus Christ has caused the Hebraic mindset to become obsolete. As previously proven, however, this is absolutely incorrect and false.

The second likely response from the Christian is that the Jews lost their chosen status, and therefore the Hebraic mindset has fallen from favor as well, replaced by God's grace. First, to say that the Jews are no longer God's chosen people is to call Him a liar. God's promises are true and eternal. If the argument becomes that the Christian has superseded the Jew ("more chosen," so to speak), how is it that the adopted child (Christian) has gained the right to change the rules of the family, that is, to alter the Law? In the beginning, Christianity was Jewish, in population, rites and strategies. Gentiles were permitted to be Christians only by abstinence from paganism (Acts 15:20-21). The fact that many Gentiles adopted into the family thereafter walked their own way was due to retention of incorrect (Gentile) doctrines, not from special dispensation from God. Second, if the validation for any portion of this claim is Paul, how then to explain his veneration of the Jew, and even of the Hebraic mindset (all previously explained)? Third, God's grace is not a grenade with which to destroy the Hebraic mindset. In fact, that grace is an integral part of Torah. One cannot destroy the vessel (Torah) without also destroying its contents (grace).

---

[28] Nevertheless, Paul errantly suggests that Gentiles should do so "by nature" rather than by actual learning.

A third and weak response from the Christian is that it's too late to remove from Christianity those Gentile things ingrained. Perhaps, but such an excuse only confesses the problem, the longevity of which does not make it right.

A fourth and even weaker response from the Christian is that the success, both financial and spiritual, of Christianity proves that God has not at all been displeased with that religion. However, this is hardly an argument, since other religions of equal force, and many of lesser consequence, have also proliferated[29].

The truth is almost certainly that Paul permitted non-Jewish Christians to retain some or many of their Gentile preferences. These preferences, incorporated into the non-Jewish sector of Christianity, soon became accepted doctrine. Any attempt to break Gentile ways for the correct Hebraic mindset was met with resentment and resistance. Therefore, the Jewish Christians, and Jews in general, became the enemies of Gentile Christianity. As the centuries passed, the church promoted its own power and revenue in part by pitting Christians against Jews. Gentile Christianity became less of religion and more of nationalistic pride. This attitude culminated in stature during the Crusades. The power of this Gentile pride was the concept of vicarious salvation, the promise of spiritual bailout for allegiance to the church. Martin Luther, who fought against the most excessive of such promises ("indulgences"), nevertheless also promulgated the "faith alone" doctrine, and fiercely battled both the Catholic Church and the Jews (the Hebraic mindset) which challenged him. Thereby, through many more centuries of interdenominational battling, and the spread of Christianity into the New World (including and especially America), the Gentile church consolidated and proliferated. Today, after so much history and growth, there is very little to motivate Gentile Christianity to correct itself to the Hebraic mindset.

14. Truth

[29] This does, however, cause one to wonder why the Jews have been not permitted by God to populate or influence as much as the Gentiles. Perhaps it is God's plan to have the smaller and meeker religion light the world.

While the church has no interest, vested or otherwise, in teaching Truth, nothing stops the individual from grasping the Hebraic mindset. From context to personal outcome, all it takes is study and focus.

Seeking Truth is, however, not without difficulty. Since most people desire security, here and hereafter, the arrogance of entitlement (spiritual bailout) is not an easy habit to break. The arrogance of superiority, that is, of numbers and powers, is also a heady fragrance, for both the Christian and the Muslim. Others are blissful in their ignorance. Many more are just plain lazy.

If you are not Jewish, you must also expect little or no peer approval or participation in your journey, as most see no benefit in your retooling. In fact, you may find opposition, or even hatred. It is a lonely, and sometimes dangerous, process. Congratulations, you are now persecuted as a Jew. But unless you convert to Judaism, even rabbinic support is liable to be thin.

Hebraic resources do, however, exist, including that of expository literature (Talmud, commentaries, and so forth) and study groups[30] (Jewish community centers, college programs, University of Truth). But beware! Once noticed, the beauty of the Truth is impossible to resist.

15. The Hebraic Bible

Is the entire Bible of an Hebraic mindset?

In Tanakh (Old Testament), God, the One God, the God of the Hebrews and the Jews, the God of Abraham, Isaac and Jacob, the God of us all, is central to every book but one. Ruth, that exception, nevertheless concerns the journey of a non-Jew within the construct of Jewish life and ethnicity, paralleled by Torah impartation. It is Hebraic.

The Gospels likewise include God at every turn[31]. Jesus, of course, was a Jew (circumcised, and having a Jewish mother), as were his apostles and

[30] Messianic Judaism may be excluded, as it includes much of the same incorrect Christian doctrine.

audience, and His mission was decidedly Jewish (to bring the lost sheep of Israel back). Christ taught doctrine only of God and Torah.

While his epistles were directed mainly to Gentiles, Paul himself was a Jew, in fact (by his words) a Pharisee. Furthermore, it cannot be denied that Paul was entreating Gentiles to remove themselves from paganism, even to be minimally Jewish (Acts 16, et al). It might be argued that as Paul progressed he grew more anti-Hebraic, and we would agree, but it nevertheless is also true that that he returned to Hebraic mindset in his maturity, that peaking in the Book of Romans. It should also not escape notice that Paul was often frustrated with his reluctant flock, a consequence he endured from having permitted pagan rites to infiltrate the true religion. His frustration denotes an ironic desire for Hebraic order among the Gentiles. Those of Paul's writings which appear distinctly anti-Jewish have likewise proven dangerous, for millennia provoking baseless Christian hatred against the Jews, to kidnap their true religion, to oust them from various nations, and to persecute them mercilessly. Shall anyone say the Jews have deserved such treatment? Paul is against such anti-Jewish boasting (Romans 11:18).

James, a Jew, touched upon Law (2:1-13, 4:11-12), and the importance of works, especially of Torah charity (2:14-26).

John, a Jew, commented strongly upon the vitality of commandments (1 John 2:1-39, 3:4, 5:2-3, et al).

Peter, a Jew, warned about false prophets who teach concerning "liberty" and yet are purveyors of corruption (2 Peter 2:18-22). While not quite a strong Torah message, it is nevertheless Hebraic mindset. Jude, a Jew, spoke likewise, though more tepidly.

---

[31] The author Luke may or may not have been a Jewish proselyte but it matters not, for his Gospel and the Book of Acts are completely Hebraic. The author John, though apt to reference "the Jews" in crass manner, was also a Jew.

The Book of Revelation is not a mystery at all. It is an expansion of Jewish eschatology, much of it originating in the Prophets (Isaiah, Daniel, Ezekiel, et al).

Finally, there is the Book of Hebrews. Though filled with things non-Hebraic, there nevertheless is at least one strong Torah message (10:26-31).

Whether or not one agrees with the Hebraic mindset, without it there is no scriptural frame of reference. It is as studying birds or stars without a guidebook. As such, finches may be erroneously identified as robins, or the constellation Orion mislabeled as Scorpio. Misinformation soon becomes incorrect doctrine. Therefore, search the scriptures with an Hebraic mindset. Be Berean. Be noble.

19. Conclusion

According to Christ, He came to bring not peace but a sword which divides (Luke 12:51). This sword is the Word of God (Hebrews 4:12, Revelation 1:16, Ephesians 6:17), that is, Torah. If Jesus brought this sword, why has it been beaten back?

Jesus died for His friends, but to be a friend of Christ one must do as He commands (John 15:13-14). If Jesus is God, those commandments are of Torah. If Jesus is not God, it must still be Torah, for "I am my Father are one" (John 10:30).

To be true religion, Christianity must therefore adopt an Hebraic mindset and reject its own incorrect doctrines, for Jesus said, "Go not into the way of the Gentiles" (Matthew 10:5) lest you hear from Him "Depart, I never knew you" (Matthew 7:23).

www.ingramcontent.com/pod-product-compliance
Ingram Content Group UK Ltd.
Pitfield, Milton Keynes, MK11 3LW, UK
UKHW041916190726
13854UKWH00003B/1270

9 781105 639999